Why Not?

(Invest in you)

Santiego Rivers

Why Not? (Invest in you)

Copyright © 2021 by Santiego Rivers

Editor – Santiego Rivers

Graphic Designer – Santiego Rivers

Interior Formatting Designer – Santiego Rivers

All rights reserved. No part of this book may be reproduced or transmitted in any form without the written permission of the author.

ISBN 978-1-7352176-8-0

There will come a time in your life that you realize that you can't fit a big dream in a small bag. The greatness within you will overpower the fears and doubts used to hold it down for far too long.

No more hiding in the shadows being afraid to shine bright because others may feel intimidated by your light that shines; let it shine.

No one else is supposed to understand your calling or know your next move but you. Make sure your calling and your next move is the best move for you and your future.

Be afraid of failure but be terrified of not living up to your potential and your standards for living your best life. Failure comes with pursuing success, so don't let it stop you from trying.

Nothing in life is permanent, so one bad chapter in your life will never tell your whole life story. Dare to be great even if you end up only being good.

Success is achieved in the effort and not the lack thereof...

Table of Content

1. Betting everything on you
2. Winners win, and losers lose
3. Excuses, Excuses, Excuses
4. What is discipline?
5. Hard work
6. Live full but die empty
7. Stop letting the Devil(s) use you
8. Your success will never be based upon a season in your life
9. Develop your action steps
10. Reasons come; first, answers come second

Betting everything on you

When it comes to achieving everything you want out of life, you must be willing to go all-in on your dreams.

There's no going in half-way when it comes to achieving your goals in life. You must be willing to commit all your time and effort to achieve success in your life.

What will it take to be successful?

It will take whatever it takes to be successful, which is why you must be willing to go all-in. There were times in my life where my desire to achieve all the things I wanted out of life was not stronger than my ability to keep fighting past my fears and doubts.

So, I quit. I quit things in my life so often that I became numb to the feeling of being a loser because, in my mind, I did not lose; I quit.

You become a loser when you stop trying to achieve success. There is no other way around this point when it comes to achieving success.

What I had to eventually do to turn my circumstances into a more favorable situation was to take a long hard look in the mirror for some self-reflection. I am a firm believer in the following quote:

If you are not getting everything you want out of life, look in the mirror and ask yourself why?

Why am I falling short on achieving my goals? Why is it easier for me to quit than continue fighting for what I say that I want? I guess for me, it was easier to say that I wished for success, but my actions did not match my words.

When times get rough, I folded quicker than a lawn chair in high wind. My reason to quit was more substantial than my desire to win which made the outcome predictable.

I wasn't willing to stand on the words of success that my mouth said I wanted to achieve.

I thought that just saying that I wanted to be successful would be enough to make my dreams a reality when it came to achieving success.

It took me many years of my life to figure out that the only way to reach my goals is by preparing myself now.

Through many failures/ attempts, you must be willing to sacrifice the person you are to become the person you want to be. There are no shortcuts or elevators on the road to success.

How bad do you want to achieve the goals you say with your mouth? If you don't want it as bad as your next breath, you will always come up short.

A person fighting for their life will always be more dangerous and hungrier than a person who is afraid to go all-in when it counts.

As I mentioned earlier; Success takes what it takes, so make sure that you are doing everything it takes to be successful.

You can't be extraordinary if you are not willing to do extra things. Nothing in your life will ever work unless you are eager to put in that work when no one is watching.

No one pays attention to the process or journey to the top of the mountain, but everybody wants to join in on your celebration when you reach the top of the hill.

No one will get up at 4 AM to watch you put in that road work. No one will be at the gym to push you at 5 AM. No one will have sympathy for you because you had to wake up 2 hours early to find the time to do a little "Extra" as you try to become an **"Extraordinary"** person.

How bad do you want it? Do you deserve it? The only thing that you will ever deserve from life is what your effort produces.

Cry if you must, but don't quit

Let the person who counted you out know that they can't count because you are still standing. Come what may, let them know you came to fight, and it is not over until you win.

Winners win, and losers lose

Everyone has a role to play in the movie. You must decide what role you will play or get stuck being cast as the loser if you don't take a stand.

You are dealing with adversity and hate is part of the process. Success requires you to learn to untie knots. No one cares about your excuses.

Excuses, Excuses, Excuses

No one cares about the reasons why you are not successful when it comes to achieving your goals.

Eighty percent of the people do not care, and the other twenty percent are glad that they are not in your situation.

Where I'm from; Hearing your excuses is your mammas' job. If you have a mom like mine, she would tell you to grow a pair and put your big boy draws on.

Life is hard, but it is fair. The only thing you should ever want from life is an opportunity to achieve your goals.

If the Most High woke you up this morning, then you have an opportunity to make the most of your day.

Create the circumstances that you want in life by going all-in on your dreams. Bet the house on you because if you don't, no one will.

Be willing to stand for something that matters. A champion's mindset is that I am the best at what I do because I am eager to do all the things you will not do.

Being the strongest or the smartest is not enough to be successful. It would be best if you had a strong work rate and the discipline to see it through. The race is not given to the swift, which is why you must be steadfast in your pursuit.

Winners do more with less because the effort that they give is their very best. Push yourself harder than anyone else will ever do. Be willing to step out of your comfort zone because nothing about being successful is comfortable.

Success begins at the end of your comfort zone, which is why success and comfort do not work together. It will take discipline to help you on your journey to success.

What is discipline?

Discipline is the bridge between who you are and who you want to become in life. It takes discipline to do the things that other people will not do to be successful.

It takes discipline to push yourself harder and further than anyone else could ever do. Only you can determine your reasons for why you put forth your effort. Your reasons are the only thing you will ever need to motivate you to keep fighting for your dreams.

Stop doing what you want to do and learn to start doing what you must do to succeed. Find your strength and learn to compensate for your weaknesses.

Until you learn to identify and address your weaknesses, you will always have excuses for why you are not living the life you desire.

Hard work

You have not because you ask not
— James 4:2-3 (KJV)

This saying has many different meanings, but you must determine what it means to you. Most people may say that this quote does not pertain to them because they always ask for everything they want from life.

People ask for money, fame, a nice car & a big house but fail to realize the one crucial thing to achieve those things. **(Hard Work)**

Faith without work is dead **– James 2:14-26**

When you ask for anything, you must first prepare to receive your blessing? How can you ask for money when you don't have a plan laid out to manage the money once you receive it?

Many people who win the lottery end up broke because they were not prepared to deal with having that type of money.

When you fail to plan, you should also plan to fail. For a dream to become a reality, you must put that dream and your plans to achieve that dream on paper. **(Vision Board)**

Write out the road map to your success and free up your mind. Give yourself a visual that will get you one step closer to reaching your goals.

It is not your mother, father, siblings, or friend's fault for you not being the best version of yourself or coming up short of your goals.

Whoever you blame for your failures will always have power over you. Take back the control you give others by putting in the needed hard work to achieve your goals.

Struggle produces the strength to move mountains which is why you must keep pushing onward and upwards.

Live full but die empty

You must be willing to sacrifice who you are for who you desire to be. To make that happen, you must be ready to use up all the gas in your tank chasing your dreams.

Put pressure on yourself and make positive changes in your life that will produce the needed changes.

Life is about taking risks. If you play it safe in life, you won't accomplish your dreams. Step out on faith and take that leap into the unknown.

If you're comfortable, you are not growing or will never accomplish the feats you are meant to overcome.

You can fail your way to success by simply putting forth the effort to succeed. When you get scared, take a deep breath and step forward. Don't worry about if it is the right time to make your move.

If you're always waiting to put your best foot forward, sometimes people never take a step forward and leave plenty of gas in their tanks that they can't take with them in death.

You don't want it, which is why you don't have it

Your mouth says one thing, but your actions tell a different story. Once you open your mouth, you tell the world who you are.

Are you a person who is willing to live the life they talk about with their action or are your words the closest you will ever get to living your dreams?

Who will you discover when your actions follow your words in the pursuit of success? If you know who you are, then you know who you are not.

There are things that only the struggle can teach you that success never will **(Trust the process)**

Where you start is not where you are supposed to finish. Life is full of regret, so make sure that the only regret that you are left with is that you didn't have another tank of gas to use chasing your dreams.

If you do what you've always done, you will always be where you have always been.

Dare to be great. Results are the only thing that counts.

Stop letting the Devil(s) use you

Your ambition will offend many people, and your success will make them very uncomfortable. Don't let it stop you from going after what you want out of life. Keep moving forward despite the opposition that you will face on your journey.

Your success in life could be one more attempt away, so you must keep trying. In the end, haters and naysayers will hate when they see you doing anything positive with your life.

Your life could be the diamond formed from all the pressure that the world put you through. Your life could be the result of how a hater is created because they let other people's negative energy become their reality.

Don't allow others to determine how you're going to act or respond to the situations/circumstances that you will face in life.

You must never forget that the enemy would not be fighting you if you were not a threat at achieving success.

Don't let others place their limitations on you. Their shortcoming or regrets should never be your burden/cross to bear.

Learn to draw the line when it comes to the things that you accept or don't from other people. Stop trying to impress the people you don't even like.

Stop relying on other people to give you your self-worth. If you rely on other people for strength, confidence, and assurance, you will always be disappointed in the end.

You must develop the mindset that "I got me."

Developing that type of mindset is the only way you will learn to take your destiny/future into your own hands.

Everyone who says that they got your "Six" doesn't honestly know what having someone "Six" means.

If you are a Christian, you know that Jesus started with 12 Disciples, but he died on the cross in the presence of only one.

Your success will never be based upon a season in your life

It is written:

- One season **David** was a shepherd, the next season, he was a king
- One season Ruth was working in the field; the next season, she owned the field
- One season **Mordecai** was sitting outside the king's palace; the next season, he was inside the palace.

These are just a few examples of many that show you that where you start in life will never be where you end up if you're willing to apply the right amount of effort.

An effort is defined by giving a vigorous or determined attempt. As long as you are willing to take care of the effort part, your success will be inevitable. Success comes with effort.

There are many times that I admit that I did not always give the effort it took for me to be successful. By not giving my very best forced me to endure long periods/seasons of unhappiness in my life.

I suffered for a long time because I spent my time blaming other people for the unhappiness in my life. It was not until I realize that both my success and failures began and ended with me. I was the culprit for my demise or amazing feats.

I had to understand how my level of success should be measured. I found out that I should judge my success level by how far I get from where I started my journey.

I needed to focus on my path and not the path of other people around me. My journey is My journey, and My success is My success. Let me repeat this in a way that will make more sense to you and your life.

Your journey is your journey, and your success is your success.

I needed to stay in my lane, and you need to do the same thing to reach the next season in your life.

Success is the by-product of the action steps you took along the way to achieve your dreams or goals.

Develop your action steps

Everyone has a dream or a goal that they would like to accomplish, but not everyone has a plan laid out on paper to help them reach their destination.

The rap artist Lil Baby wanted to be a recording artist. The plan that he laid out included him devoting his time, money & dedication to his craft.

He paid another rap artist to write rhymes for him to go into the studio and practice the delivery of his verses.

His first step in achieving his goal was deciding to dedicate himself to his craft. His next step was finding someone who could help him develop his skills. The third step included him investing in his dream/goal. His fourth step included him taking the time to practice his craft while everyone around him was busy getting into trouble.

Lil baby had dreams for his life. He knew that a goal without work was pointless, so he worked hard.

He had to change the person he was to become the type of person he wanted to become. Success does not happen overnight. Success is a process that is continuously evolving. The following is an analogy that I like to use to explain what success should be measured by.

A tree is judged by the fruit it bears. It is not judged by its' effort or lack thereof. Did the tree produce ripe fruits?

Your actions steps are continually changing. Once you remove one of your actions steps off your dream board, you must replace it with another to help keep you moving forward.

There will be times when you must put back a previous action step because there will be many setbacks on the road to success.

Don't get discouraged by the setbacks you encounter on your path. Stay focused on the task at hand. When it comes to achieving success, remember the following.

The harder that you attack your action steps, the closer you will get to achieving your goals.

Reasons come; first, answers come second

What is your reason for why? Your why is the reason you need to find the courage to invest everything you have into yourself.

You can't afford to not invest in yourself. Losing is too expensive, and the only thing success cost is unsuccessful people disliking you.

Are you willing to pay that price to achieve your goals?

I told you earlier to stop trying to impress people you don't like or do not like you for the person you are.

The best experience in my life came from me hitting rock bottom. Once you reach the lowest point in your life, you discover who you are as a person and who you can count on when the chips are down.

Having nothing makes you hungry. Have you been hungry in your life? The sound and pain from an empty stomach push pride to the side in search of your next meal. You must do whatever it takes to feed that beast at the bottom of your stomach.

This is the same principle when trying to achieve success in your life when you hit rock bottom.

Hitting rock bottom has produced many winners and, unfortunately, many failures because they stop fighting for what they wanted out of life.

When you are tempted to quit the fight for success, you must remember why you started to fight for victory in the first place.

Life teaches us lessons rather we want them or not. You will need a strong mind and heart to endure all the tasks that life will bring your way.

Many people start their journey to success, but many give up before they cross the finish line. The path to success is lonely, but the reward for achieving your goals is priceless, especially for the people you will inspire by your success.

Be the first person in your family to become successful or continue the tradition taught to you by your family.

Why Not Invest in You?

www.ingramcontent.com/pod-product-compliance
Lightning Source LLC
Chambersburg PA
CBHW071014160426
43193CB00012B/2056